"To the one experiencing unrelenting chronic pain or emotional distress, this book is a comforting first-line prescription for rehearsing biblical truth. Each chapter concludes with practical applications for the sufferer's toolbox. All of us, whether sufferers or comforters living east of Eden, can benefit from these reminders of God's providential care."

Julia Breuninger, RN, Member Care, OC International

"'We have this treasure in jars of clay' (2 Corinthians 4:7). But what happens when our 'jar of clay' becomes irreparably broken . . . when the hurt won't heal? With compassion and wisdom born from his personal struggle with chronic illness, Craig guides the reader to a place of spiritual flourishing in the midst of unrelenting pain. The treasure of our hope in Christ makes all the difference!"

Pamela Gannon, RN, ACBC Certified Biblical Counselor; coauthor of *In the Aftermath: Past the Pain of Childhood Sexual Abuse*

"Sometimes when the darkness of persistent suffering threatens to disorient and overwhelm us, we need a sure guide—a hand in the dark. In *When the Hurt Won't Heal*, Craig Svensson offers chronic sufferers a steadying hand to help guide them out of the gloom. His hand has been steadied by careful Christian reflection on his own chronic suffering. Highly recommended."

Mark Talbot, Associate Professor of Philosophy Emeritus, Wheaton College; author of the Suffering and the Christian Life series

"In *When the Hurt Won't Heal*, Craig Svensson shares his journey of physical suffering and loss, describing how God is bringing him through it and how God will carry us through suffering as well. This book will be a great resource for my patients and for counselees who are facing pain and problems that will not go away. I highly recommend it!"

Charles Hodges, MD, Family Physician; fellow, Association of Certified Biblical Counselors (ACBC); counselor and instructor, Faith Biblical Counseling Ministries; editor of *The Christian Counselor's Medical Desk Reference*

"Dr. Svensson is in a very unique position to provide comfort and counsel on this important subject. What I especially appreciated was the wonderful balance of rich theology with practical guidelines for everyday life. Readers will benefit greatly from this warm, wise presentation of important biblical truth."

Stephen Viars, Senior Pastor, Faith Church, Lafayette, IN; board member, Association of Certified Biblical Counselors (ACBC); author of *Do You Believe What God Says About You?*

WHEN THE HURT WON'T HEAL

WHEN THE HURT WON'T HEAL

LIVING WITH CHRONIC ILLNESS

Craig K. Svensson

newgrowthpress.com

New Growth Press, Greensboro, NC 27401
newgrowthpress.com

Cover Design: Studio Gearbox, studiogearbox.com
Interior Typesetting and eBook: Lisa Parnell, lparnellbookservices.com

ISBN: 978-1-64507-472-4 (Print)
ISBN: 978-1-64507-473-1 (eBook)

Library of Congress Cataloging-in-Publication Data
Names: Svensson, Craig K., author.
Title: When the hurt won't heal : living with chronic illness / Craig K. Svensson.
Description: Greensboro, NC : New Growth Press, [2024] | Series: Ask the Christian counselor
Identifiers: LCCN 2024012955 (print) | LCCN 2024012956 (ebook) | ISBN 9781645074724 (print) | ISBN 9781645074731 (ebook)
Subjects: LCSH: Diseases—Religious aspects—Christianity. | Medical care—Religious aspects—Christianity. | Counseling—Religious aspects—Christianity. | Suffering—Religious aspects—Christianity.
Classification: LCC BV4460 .S75 2024 (print) | LCC BV4460 (ebook) | DDC 259/.41—dc23/eng/20240520
LC record available at https://lccn.loc.gov/2024012955
LC ebook record available at https://lccn.loc.gov/2024012956

Printed in the United States of America

31 30 29 28 27 26 25 24 1 2 3 4 5

CONTENTS

INTRODUCTION

Not long ago, an alarm on a piece of lab equipment across from my university office began blaring, and the staff was unavailable to stop it. Seconds turned into minutes and minutes into hours as the alarm droned on. As the beeping of the alarm continued in the background, I grew unsettled. The incessant *beep-beep-beep* became so irritating that I could no longer concentrate on my work. I had to exit the building to find relief.

But what if my circumstances had been different? What if I had no path for escape? The nonstop irritation made it challenging to accomplish my work, and yet it needed to be done. Could I find a way to work through the constantly blaring siren without losing my mind? Like a seemingly unrelenting alarm that grates on the nerves, there are many who live with an enduring trial, an affliction that won't go away.

Some people suffer from ongoing physical pain. Others are plagued with unending dizziness or fatigue, tingling in the ears or vision that is continually blurred, or a host of other symptoms that are like a slow grinder chipping away at their body. Their health is impaired and life is no longer normal. Dreams have been dashed and simple activities of daily life are no longer so simple. They live with an ailment for which there is no cure.

There are also those who live with the haunting memories of past trauma, terrors that are frequently relived and renew the harm. Still others experience repeated periods of descending into a darkness of mind that won't lift, robbing them of joy and hope. There are also those who are frequently gripped with overwhelming anxiety about the future, leaving them feeling unable to cope with the vicissitudes of life.

Perhaps you find yourself in one of the above conditions. If so, I wrote this book for you. In particular, this book can help you navigate the hard challenge of living with a hurt that won't heal, a pain that persists, or a darkness that won't dispel. If you are trying to navigate life with an endless trial, the chapters ahead will help you find the path to flourish spiritually despite the ongoing pain, fear, or darkness.

Or perhaps you are seeking to come alongside and help those who are suffering from a chronic illness or a mental/emotional struggle. My hope is that the chapters ahead will help you do so with wisdom and compassion. Scripture reminds us that two are better than one while on this journey of life (Ecclesiastes 4:9–10). You can be a source of encouragement to others who are living with ongoing affliction. But if you are to avoid the errors of Job's three friends, you must tread carefully. Job's friends began well, as they sat with him and entered into his pain. They erred when they sought to uncover the *why* behind his suffering. If you are seeking to comfort a sufferer, my hope is that the pages ahead will equip you to do so with wisdom and grace. If you are willing to sit with sufferers, you can be a source of comfort and help.

The content within these pages arises from my experience of living with several incurable ailments and the tragic loss of my youngest son. My journey with chronic illness began during my first year of marriage, when frequent episodes of knee–buckling intestinal cramping and lengthy periods in the bathroom led me to seek the help of several specialists, who ultimately diagnosed a rare form of colitis. For the next fifteen years, our life was deeply impacted by flare-ups that caused me to miss important events in our children's lives and forced my wife to become adept at preparing meals for a husband with an increasingly limited diet. She lived with the weight of watching her husband repeatedly writhing on the floor in pain after dinner and fearful that something she served was the cause.

In the providence of God, a significant measure of relief finally came when I spent several days doing consulting work for the National Institutes of Health and was seated next to a specialist investigating the same rare form of colitis. He experimented with a drug used for a different purpose. Several patients responded positively, and he suggested I give it a trial. I did so and went from an average of four attacks a week to only four in the first four months.

Sadly, finding some relief from colitis coincided with a back injury that left me in excruciating pain. My world became increasingly small as numerous specialists were unable to find any intervention to relieve the agony. The first decade of living with chronic pain was, in many ways, life–altering. The unceasing siren of pain in my back made sitting nearly impossible and limited my physical activity in many ways. Vacation plans were discarded and chores on the homestead went undone. I gained a reputation as the guy who always stood during worship services, concerts, airplane travel, and meetings of every sort.

Nearing the end of my first decade with chronic pain, I lost part of my vision in one eye during a lengthy plane ride over the Pacific Ocean. This event, combined with additional neurological symptoms, led me to join the more than one million Americans living with multiple sclerosis. Relapses over the years have left me with areas of my body that persistently tingle or burn.

I understand what it feels like when you live with a hurt that won't heal. The spiritual, emotional, and relational challenges that arise when living with an incurable ailment are very real. Persistent physical illness tests our spiritual well-being. Like Job, I came to see how hard it is to thrive spiritually when you are robbed of your physical health.

I trained as a pharmacist-scientist and have spent my professional life as a professor and university administrator. My clinical training included managing the care of patients with a variety of chronic illnesses. Through the years, I've been a part of preparing countless young people to be the pharmacists, physicians, nurses, and physician assistants of the future. I've taught about pain medicine and other interventions to relieve human suffering. But neither my training nor professional experience prepared me for the tough questions I face as a patient living with incurable illness.

Where is God when pain piles upon pain? Is there a purpose behind it all? How can we forestall the emotional roller coaster an enduring trial can produce? Can we grow spiritually while physical limitations shrink our world? How do we find help for such perplexing questions when easy answers will not suffice?

These experiences and the spiritual dilemma they exposed have driven me to Scripture and to seek the wisdom of those more seasoned in living with an enduring affliction. I have also had the privilege of sharing this content in formal settings with biblical counselors and people living with chronic illness. Their feedback has helped refine both my thinking and this content. My prayer is that the Lord will use it to help you know the fullness of joy that Jesus offers.

A journey through life with chronic illness is like traveling on a road with dangerous ditches on both sides. Swerve to the left and you'll descend into the depths of despondency. Swerve to the right and your illness will become the focus of your life and the core of your identity. Neither ditch is a place we want to land. To avoid doing so, we must recognize the danger—understanding the spiritual challenges and the destructive direction our hearts are inclined to travel.

But here's the key message: the good news of Jesus Christ changes *everything*, including how we live in the face of chronic illness. The joy that Jesus promises is not only for those who live with good health. It's also for those facing various types of enduring trials, including chronic illness. I hope to help you find the path to that joy.

Chapter 1

FINDING HELP IN THE JOURNEY[1]

After months of constant back pain that upended my life, a series of tests ordered by a spinal specialist provided me with hope that I might discover the cause of my pain and a path to alleviate it. But hope disappeared like smoke with the frank assessment of this learned physician: "There is no clear cause and there is really nothing more we can do for you. You will just have to learn to live with it." Yet he gave me no insight for exactly how I was supposed to do that.

As I left his office, a darkness I had never before experienced engulfed me. The thought of living with incessant pain for the foreseeable future seemed unbearable. All hope was dashed, and there was nothing but darkness on the horizon. As I sat alone in my car in the parking lot, with debilitating pain in my back and even worse hurt in my heart, I felt emotionally paralyzed. I realized I was descending into a dangerous darkness of soul, from which I needed help to escape. How could I live for Jesus in the face of inescapable pain?

In what might be the most memorized of the Psalms, David declares, "Even though I walk through the valley of the shadow of death, I will fear no evil, for you are with me; your rod and your staff, they comfort me" (Psalm 23:4).

Often, we and others are powerless to remove the darkness. We cannot ascend out of the "valley of the shadow of death." The pain will not cease, health will not be restored, depression will not lift, and traumatic terrors of the night will not disappear. But there is help *within* the valley. We need to see that God is there with us in the valley. He is not just randomly out there somewhere, but he is with us in the place of darkness. Thus, we need practical tools to help us see truth when all has gone dark.

Figure 1 illustrates the helps we can use when darkness overtakes: the Word, music, community, and biblical counsel. They provide the means by which we can see God through the fog. They represent God-ordained paths where we can find help when we're in a world of hurt.

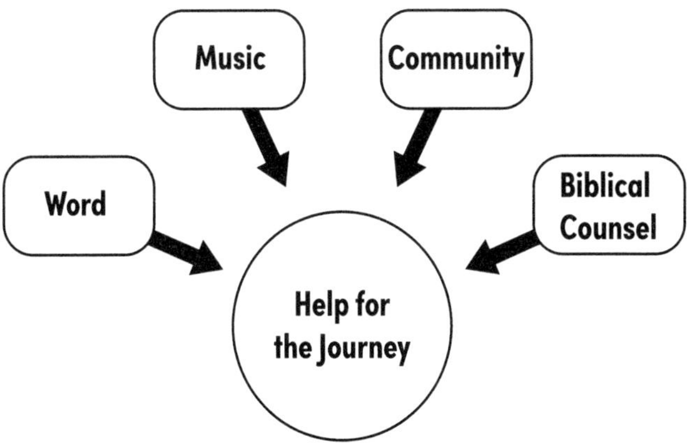

Figure 1. Means of Help for Living With an Enduring Affliction

But here's a key point: it is best to have these in place *before* our vision of God is obscured by trouble. Stumbling around in darkness looking for them is much harder. Those who live with an enduring trial are going to experience difficult days and need a plan to see them through such periods. Those living with chronic pain will face days when the physical challenge of ordinary life seems unbearable. For others, a mental darkness descends with an unexplainable regularity—taking their mind into places they should not dwell. It is essential to develop a recovery plan for the dark moments in life, especially when living with a lifelong affliction.

Nevertheless, if darkness descends when you are unprepared, these helps are accessible to you. They might be harder to put in place in the midst of trouble, but like a first-aid kit, you can grab them if you know where to find them.

THE WORD: PROMISES TO ANCHOR OUR SOULS

The psalmist declares, "Your word is a lamp to my feet and a light to my path" (Psalm 119:105). What better place to turn when darkness descends than the Bible? But the Bible is a big book. A random opening of its pages when in need might not be the best strategy. Far better to be prepared by knowing where to turn when you need light to navigate through troubled territory. Memorizing passages of the promise of his presence will allow us to speak truth to ourselves when we feel abandoned by God (e.g., Psalm 55:22; Psalm 121; 1 Corinthians 10:13). In addition, marking key psalms to turn to gives us truth to draw upon when trouble comes.

For example, saints in sore affliction often find it hard to pray. This is a time to let Psalms be a template for our prayers, especially psalms of lament. Lament has two simple parts: (1) talk to God about your feelings, and then (2) talk to your feelings about God. In other words, express your agony to God. Voice the deepest feelings of your heart in prayer. Then speak truth to your heart. Settle your soul with solid truth. Psalm 13 illustrates this well when the psalmist gives voice to his pain (vv. 1–4), then steadies himself with sure truths (vv. 5–6):

How long, O Lord? Will you forget me forever?
How long will you hide your face from me?
How long must I take counsel in my soul
and have sorrow in my heart all the day?
How long shall my enemy be exalted over me?
Consider and answer me, O Lord my God;
light up my eyes, lest I sleep the sleep of death,
lest my enemy say, "I have prevailed over him,"
lest my foes rejoice because I am shaken.
But I have trusted in your steadfast love;
my heart shall rejoice in your salvation.
I will sing to the Lord,
because he has dealt bountifully with me.

This is a pattern for us to emulate. Our emotions are God-given, but feelings can also lead us astray, for they are tainted by a sin-stained heart. This is why rehearsing truth is so important. It might *feel* like God has abandoned us, but we know he has promised that he never will. In the words of David above, he expresses his resolve to act on the truth he knows, not the feelings he experiences in the moment.

This practice of preaching to yourself, speaking biblical truth to our troubled hearts, is an essential step to steadying our souls in the midst of affliction. And it is a truth exemplified in many places in Scripture besides the Psalms. For example, the writer of Lamentations poetically expressed his anguish at the destruction of Jerusalem. Amid the rubble of the city and his life, he declares, "My endurance has perished; so has my hope from the Lord" (3:18). But the troubled prophet doesn't stay there. He goes on to speak truth to his heart:

But this I call to mind,
    and therefore I have hope:
The steadfast love of the Lord never ceases;
    his mercies never come to an end;
they are new every morning;
    great is your faithfulness.
"The Lord is my portion," says my soul,
    "therefore I will hope in him."
    (Lamentations 3:21–24)

What gave the writer of Lamentations hope was calling to mind sure truths, especially the enduring reality of the Lord's steadfast love.

Other psalms take our eyes off our trouble and focus them on our gracious Creator (e.g., Psalms 8 and 19). We should each have a small set of psalms to which we turn in difficult times. Praying through these can bring much help when we are in a world of hurt.

In the providence of God, we also can find truth we are not particularly looking for in our time of need. If we have made a habit of systematic daily Bible reading, the scheduled reading will sometimes contain a nugget of truth that is helpful for our need in the moment. The benefit of working our way through a daily Bible reading plan extends beyond giving us a comprehensive view of the story of the Bible; it also provides a way for us to find help for the day. I can't count the number of times my daily devotional time led me to the truth I needed for the struggle of that particular day.

MUSIC: SONGS OF SACRED TRUTHS

Gospel-saturated music is a marvelous gift that is a balm to the soul and a beacon in darkness. When darkness gripped King Saul, he was refreshed by the music of David

(1 Samuel 16:14–23). When the sons of Korah, the worship leaders of Israel, were led away into the Babylonian captivity, they penned one of the most reassuring of all the psalms (Psalm 42). What was the last thing Jesus and his disciples did before they went to the Mount of Olives—the place of his deep anguish—on that fateful night? They sang a hymn (Matthew 26:30).

Songs of biblical truth can steady our souls; they anchor us to truth in life's storms. We should all have a few go-to songs that help us see God in times of darkness. Joni Eareckson Tada's book, *Songs of Suffering: 25 Hymns and Devotions for Weary Souls*, has been a helpful resource to many sufferers.

Music has a way of penetrating the heart with a depth unmatched by the spoken or written word. Those who have raised children have surely experienced times when a song stilled a crying child. Many of us have watched the calmness that songs of hope brought to a loved one in precious moments before death's grip seized them. And music can wonderfully still our troubled souls in unsettled times when pain, fear, or darkness have gripped us.

Often when grief over the death of my beloved son, Eric, tightened its grip on my heart, songs such as "He Will Hold Me Fast" and "In the Valley" brought peace and hope. Their words stimulated the resolve to go forth and do what needed to be done, to trudge through the darkness in the assurance of my Lord's presence and care. The grief did not disappear, but neither did it paralyze. Not knowing when a wave of grief would threaten to overwhelm, it was helpful to have such songs in my pocket. While smartphones can make us dumb, they also allow us to have songs of gospel truth readily available to lift our souls in troubled times. Akin to stocking a first aid kit with bandages, modern electronic devices allow us to curate a few key hymns or spiritual songs.

COMMUNITY: OTHERS TO WALK WITH US

It is dangerous to walk through trials alone. As the Preacher of Ecclesiastes points out, "Two are better than one, because they have a good reward for their toil. For if they fall, one will lift up his fellow. But woe to him who is alone when he falls and has not another to lift him up!" (4:9–10).

We have been created to flourish in community, especially the community of the saints. When we place our faith in Jesus, we become a part of his body—the church. The book of Acts and the Epistles portray the local church as a visible, interdependent collection of followers of Jesus who give themselves to one another. My wife and I have the privilege of being part of a local church whose members display such sacrificial care for one another. We have received, shared in, and watched the support of believers toward those in all types of trials. I cannot imagine walking through our trials alone, nor does our Lord want us to try.

But you cannot experience this help if you are not a part of a local church or if you only live on the periphery of a congregation. People can also be very involved in a local church, yet close to no one. You must not confuse busyness with true relationship. You must be willing to link yourself arm-in-arm with other believers, which requires getting close. A willingness to be open and vulnerable with others is essential to developing the type of relationships that can help you in difficult trials. And yes, it will be messy at times, because we who live in frail flesh will fail one another. It is sadly inevitable. Yet if we allow this to prevent us from drawing close to other believers, none will be there to lift us up when we fall. So find believers to link arms with. Weave your life with the lives of others. Then, when trouble comes, others will be there to help you.

Experiencing the benefit of community also requires humility to serve and be served. Our pride often makes us resistant to seek or receive help. I was convicted of this years ago while teaching through the "one anothers" of Scripture (e.g., comfort one another, serve one another, exhort one another). My brethren in the local congregation cannot be all the body of Christ is meant to be if I am unwilling to make my need known. Similarly, they cannot fulfill their duty to me as a fellow believer if I am too proud to accept their help.

Some saints with the spiritual gift of mercy serve their suffering brothers or sisters in Christ best in practical ways. We have a dear friend who spends much of her time driving others to their medical appointments, some of which are more than an hour away. This simple help is of great benefit to the recipients, and it's how she serves the Lord. But she could not serve in this way if others were unwilling to receive her help. Other folks delight in providing meals or performing physical work to lighten the load of their brothers and sisters in Christ.

While it is true that some abuse the generosity of others and none of us want to become an undue burden to others, we should realize that sharing our needs gives opportunity to others to fulfill the call of Jesus to love one another. In so doing, we are giving visible witness to a watching world that we are his disciples. A community of believers who sacrifices time, treasure, and talent for one another is a powerful witness to a world in desperate need of the light of the gospel.

Another source of help from the community of believers is the collective power of prayer. Asking other saints to struggle for us in prayer while we wrestle with our hearts should be part of our response to trials. If we believe that the prayers of the righteous accomplish much (James 5:16), we should be quick to seek prayers when gripped in darkness. We all need a list of faithful prayer warriors to whom we can turn in a time of need. Doing so should be second nature for us.

Perhaps as you read the words above, you realize you are not part of a community of believers devoted to one another. If this is your situation, realize that the transforming power of community can begin with you. Find a need and fill it. Involve yourself in serving others. As you do so, you will find a bond developing between you and those you serve or serve with. Moreover, as you give yourself to meeting the needs of others, you will take your mind off yourself and your troubles. There is no better way to guard against self-pity and self-centeredness (which we all struggle with) than sacrificially giving ourselves to others.

BIBLICAL COUNSEL: WISDOM FROM EXPERIENCED SAINTS

Sometimes flashlights and candles do not provide enough light when electricity is lost. We need more intense help, such as a friend with a mobile generator. In the same way, we also need to know where to turn when our usual spiritual aids prove insufficient for the darkness we face. There is no shame in seeking more specialized help when in sore affliction, any more than there is in seeking help for a physical problem that strikes our body.

How do you know when you need more specialized help? First, realize we all need spiritual help all the time. We all need believers who can speak truth into our lives on a regular basis. Truth be told, we are sometimes slow to see our own spiritual needs, and others who do life with us can often see troubled areas to which we are blind. This is yet another blessing of living in a community of believers and doing life together. This means a willingness to take seriously the words of others when they lovingly express their concern about our spiritual well-being. As we have watched others struggle in small groups we have led over the years, my wife and I have experienced a variety of reactions when we recommend that they need more structured help, such as biblical counseling. Some have reacted with offense and continued to wallow. Others have accepted the advice and sought counsel, finding the structured help they needed to settle them in their journey.

Second, when you are feeling overwhelmed and unable to fulfill your varied responsibilities in life, it is time to seek help. If you find yourself losing joy in things you normally enjoy or withdrawing from activities with others for weeks on end, this is a sign that you would benefit from another believer coming alongside and helping you in the midst of a rough patch.

But to whom do you turn in your time of need? A good starting point might be a seasoned saint in your small group. Someone with whom you have an established relationship can often speak into your life more readily than others. Also, does your church or one nearby have trained biblical counselors who can combine experience and knowledge of the Word to bring light into the darkness? In addition, pastors/elders can often provide counsel or direct you to those who can. Sometimes people are hesitant to involve leaders in their time of need, fearing they will be a burden to their pastors/elders. But making them aware of your struggle enables them to fulfill their calling to care for the flock over which God has given them care.

We all know to call 911 in the event of a physical emergency. It is foolish not to call when an emergency arises. In the same way, we should not hesitate to seek help in the face of a spiritual emergency.

It is inevitable that those living with an enduring affliction will face times of darkness, doubt, and even despair. But we can prepare for such times. Most importantly, we need to remember our gracious Lord will be our help in such times of need. As the psalmist reminds us, "For he delivers the needy when he calls, the poor and him who has no helper. He has pity on the weak and the needy, and saves the lives of the needy" (Psalm 72:12–13).

QUESTIONS FOR REFLECTION AND APPLICATION

1. When was the last time you read through the book of Psalms? If doing so is not already on your reading plan, consider regularly reading through Psalms to gain insight into how the psalmists addressed suffering in their own lives. Keep a journal to write down key truths you learn and psalms you want to return to in the future.

2. Create a playlist on your smartphone with songs you can listen to when facing dark times. If you are part of a small group, ask others what songs they have found especially helpful in dark times.

Chapter 2
LEARNING TO TRUST THE PROVIDENCE OF GOD

I am a planner. I don't make a to-do list. Instead, I schedule my tasks in my electronic calendar. I even plan time for the unplanned that inevitably crops up during the day. My assistant once quipped that my workday was planned in five-minute increments. Not surprisingly, I struggle when my well-laid plans get cast aside by something unexpected that consumes a substantial portion of the day. I must battle within myself to remember that the Lord is actually in control of my calendar and trust in his control.

Likewise, my life plan did not include three incurable ailments. Living with enduring physical suffering was not part of my ambition. When each ailment arrived, I knew God had the power to make it disappear. But he didn't. Despite the earnest prayers of my faithful wife and friends, more pain arrived rather than relief. That inevitably led to the most perplexing question of all: Why?

When God does not bring relief from suffering, followers of Jesus often find themselves struggling with the *why* behind their calamity. Not just why has trouble come, but why has *relief* from that trouble *not* come? *Does God not care about my suffering? Is he unaware of what I am going through? Is he unable to take it away? Am I failing to learn what I should from the affliction? Is God angry with me?*

At its core, these and related questions touch on our relationship with God himself. Consider examples of anguished cries from the heart in the Psalter:

> How long, O LORD? Will you forget me forever?
> How long will you hide your face from me?
> How long must I take counsel in my soul
> and have sorrow in my heart all the day?
> How long shall my enemy be exalted over me?
> (Psalm 13:1–2)

> Out of the depths I cry to you, O LORD!
> O Lord, hear my voice!
> Let your ears be attentive
> to the voice of my pleas for mercy! (Psalm 130:1–2)

The agony of the psalmist is self-evident and reminds us that feeling abandoned by or distanced from God is a common experience for those living with trouble that won't cease. Unrelenting suffering can threaten our sense of the Lord's presence. A friend living with an ongoing ailment recently said to me, "I am having a hard time seeing Jesus in the midst of my suffering."

Despite such feelings, the reality is that Jesus will never leave us or forsake us; he is with us always (Hebrews 13:5; Matthew 28:20). So where do we find stability and hope when troubling circumstances create a sense of abandonment? It begins with learning to trust the providence of God in every circumstance.

WHAT IS PROVIDENCE?

Though many have provided definitions of God's providence, perhaps none has done so with greater clarity than the writers of the Belgic Confession (Article 13): "We believe that this good God, after creating all things, did not abandon them to chance or fortune but leads and governs them according to his holy will, in such a way that nothing happens in this world without God's orderly arrangement."[2]

This portion of the confession communicates the consistent message of Scripture from Genesis to Revelation: our Creator is in control of all things. As such, he works all things to achieve his purposes. Nothing happens out of his control, and all that happens accomplishes his sovereign purposes, even when it does not look that way to us.

To the nonexpert, hurricanes and tornadoes seem to be examples of chaos. But in the eyes of meteorologists, they are highly ordered events whose movements are comprehendible. The diverse impact of an earthquake on a single city block might appear to be random. Nevertheless, earthquake experts tell us that the collapse of one building and the endurance of adjacent buildings is quite understandable if you know about structural engineering and the effect of shifting tectonic plates. Similarly, events in our lives might seem to be a matter of being in the wrong place at the wrong time or the cruel luck of the draw. But they are not. All are ordered by our gracious Creator.

Consider the response of our Lord Jesus to the disciples' question about the reason for a man's blindness: "As he passed by, he saw a man blind from birth. And his disciples asked him, 'Rabbi, who sinned, this man or his parents, that he was born blind?' Jesus answered, 'It was not that this man sinned, or his parents, but that the works of God might be displayed in him'" (John 9:1–3). Did you catch the cause of this man's blindness? It was not the curse of genes or disease. It was not a tragic embryological error. Nor was it sin on his part or his parents'. It was, in the providence of God, so "that the works of God might be displayed in him." There was a divine purpose behind his handicap from birth.

This man lived for years in blindness. He never saw the tender look of his mother, the beauty of a sunrise, or the majestic glow of a starlit night. He was an outcast, reduced to begging for sustenance. Importantly, his deprivation for all those years was for this singular moment—the moment Jesus would arrive and glorify his Father through the miraculous act of giving sight to one born blind. His blindness and the limitations it caused were part of God's unfolding redemptive plan.

Long ago, this passage from John helped me to put aside the question of *why* regarding my own accumulated ailments. Prior to Jesus arriving on the scene, there is no way this man born blind could have understood the plan and purpose of God for his suffering. God is doing a myriad of things that I am unaware of and unable to comprehend. Knowing this, I do not need to know the *why* behind my own affliction because I know who is behind it all. And I know he will work it out for my good (Romans 8:28). He will do the same in your affliction, whatever it might be.

The Lord accomplishes his work even through the evil deeds of men. Consider the experience of Joseph, the favored son of Jacob. His brothers sold him into slavery because of their jealousy. Yet when Joseph confronted them after he ascended to power in Egypt, he could say, "Do not fear, for am I in the place of God? As for you, you meant evil against me, but God meant it for good, to bring it about that many people should be kept alive, as they are today" (Genesis 50:19–20).

Yes, God can even use the evil acts of others for good. How can that be? Because "nothing happens in this world without God's orderly arrangement" (Belgic Confession, Article 13). The purposes of God cannot be thwarted. Neither the schemes of devils nor men will prevent his plan from unfolding. God is never surprised by what happens in his creation, and that includes the troubling circumstances that upend our lives. They are all part of his grand design.

It's one thing to acknowledge that all that happens is part of God's providence, his unfolding plan for our lives. But can it settle my troubled heart? Can this knowledge bring comfort in our times of turmoil? If so, why and how?

WHY IS PROVIDENCE A COMFORTING TRUTH?

The providence of God is not a comforting truth simply because it assures me that someone is in control and has a purpose in all that happens. An all-powerful despot who pulls the levers of life would not be a source of comfort. The providence of God is a source of comfort because of who he has shown himself to be. He is not simply omnipotent and omniscient. He is more than just sovereign over all. The one who is all these things is also my *Father*. I am a child of the master of the universe, the one who ordains all things. It is my Abba, Father, who has charted this path for me.

No one in the narrative of the Bible makes more frequent reference to our Creator as Father than his beloved Son. Jesus taught us to pray to God as our Father (Matthew 6:9). He urged us not to be anxious because our heavenly Father knows of our needs and will meet them (Matthew 6:25–33). He reminded us that it is our Father who brings sunshine and rain (Matthew 5:45). Our Father sees everything that occurs in secret, but rewards in the open (Matthew 6:1–6). Consequently, we can freely come to him and make our requests with confidence in his gracious care (Matthew 7:7–11). Ultimately, Jesus will come for us and bring us into our Father's house, where there will be no more pain or sorrow (John 14:1–6).

The comfort brought by the providence of God comes because of my relationship with him. It is rooted in the fact that through Jesus, I have been brought into his forever family. And far better than the best of earthly fathers, my heavenly Father cares for me more than I can even imagine. His care never fails. Nor is there any circumstance, however troubling it might be, that will remove me from his loving care. I am forever held in his all-powerful and tender hands.

HOW CAN I LEARN TO TRUST GOD IN THE MIDST OF SUFFERING?

Understanding the providence of God is a matter for the head, but trust is a matter of the heart. Knowing God is my Father gives reasons for trust, but the confidence to rest in that trust is built through times of testing. In other words, the trustworthiness of God as my Father is proven and strengthened experientially.

Think of the people in your life whom you trust most. Why do they have your confidence? Isn't it because they have proven themselves to be trustworthy through various circumstances? The same occurs in our walk with God. As our journey with him progresses, our confidence in his care grows as we experience evidence of that care. These experiences give us the basis for trust when things happen that we do not understand. This reality also points us to a key step in finding comfort in trials: *rehearse past experiences of God's care in trials*.

The Lord established a rhythmic calendar of celebrations for Israel to remember God's provision through their times of testing in Egypt and their wandering in the wilderness (e.g., Leviticus 23). Each celebration was to strengthen their trust in the Lord's faithfulness to them. Likewise, when we rehearse experiences of God's provision through times of testing in our own lives, it strengthens our trust in his future care.

But here's the rub: trust will be shallow when trials have been few. If you have not seen or experienced God's care through prior times of difficulty, the reservoir from which to draw is limited. This is why it is no surprise that new Christians tend to struggle more than seasoned saints in times of testing. This is also one reason why living life in a community of believers (the local church) is of such importance. In doing so, we can watch and listen to the testimony of others.

For the generation of Israelites delivered out of Egypt, festivals would have, in some sense, been reliving their experience. Each would have reminded them of the trail they had traveled and brought to mind God's presence and care during their times of testing. For subsequent generations, the stories of their ancestors would have given credible testimony to God's faithfulness. In other words, the experience of their ancestors would have been a means to strengthen the trust of subsequent generations.

Mature saints, those who have walked with the Lord for some time, can serve a similar role in the lives of those who are young in the faith, as well as those who are not so young. Indeed, they are specifically called to do so: "Blessed be the God and Father of our Lord Jesus Christ, the Father of mercies and God of all comfort, who comforts us in all our affliction, *so that we may be able to comfort those who are in any affliction*, with the comfort with which we ourselves are comforted by God" (2 Corinthians 1:3–4, emphasis added).

One reason we experience comfort in trials is to equip us to comfort others in their times of testing. For this reason, those who are struggling in their trials should look to fellow believers as a source of strength. Their experiences help us see the faithfulness of God to his children.

If you are young in the faith, open your eyes. Watch how mature Christians endure their times of testing. Ask them what enables them to endure. Listen to them recount how the Lord has cared for them in times of trouble. And remember, you have the same heavenly Father. He will also care for you. On that, you can bank your trust.

QUESTIONS FOR REFLECTION AND APPLICATION

1. How have you seen God's providential care in your life until now? Journal or share with a friend some of the ways you have seen God work in your life in the past.

2. Choose a passage on God's providence cited in this chapter and memorize or meditate on it this week, especially focusing on the comfort it provides.

3. Ask a Christian brother or sister this week to share with you how God has shown his providential hand in their life.

Chapter 3

DESIRING GOD MORE THAN RELIEF

Early in my journey with chronic illness, I earnestly pleaded for relief, as did my dear wife. As weeks turned into months and months into years, it was obvious that our prayers for relief were not granted. I then faced a perplexing question: Should I stop asking for healing? When a second incurable ailment joined the journey, I found myself wondering whether pleading for healing was the right response. By the time disease number three joined the others, the question of whether or not to pray for healing was no longer a struggle for me. But perhaps it remains an unsettled issue for you.

How should we pray when plagued with a persistent affliction? Do we endlessly pound the door of heaven for relief? Is removal of the cause of our suffering the only path to flourishing in life? Instead of pursuing the passing of our hardship, whether that be the restoration of health or removal of the darkness that haunts us, should we be praying for something else?

The pursuits of our hearts are always important. If we seek for the wrong thing, our longings will ruin us. Thus, what we pursue when in the crucible of affliction is crucial. Our pleadings in prayer during times of suffering not only reveal the deepest longings of our hearts; they also *mold* our hearts. They shape our thoughts and affections. And the affections of our hearts are what drive our actions.

An enduring trial can make us self-focused, even in our prayers. Though we might be praying more than ever, those prayers are easily misaligned. Because suffering often distorts our perspective, we tend to place our longing for relief above all else.

There is remarkable insight on this matter from Elihu in the book of Job.[3] He says to his fellow debaters,

> "Because of the multitude of oppressions people cry out; they call for help because of the arm of the mighty. But none says, 'Where is God my Maker, who gives songs in the night, who teaches us more than the beasts of the earth and makes us wiser than the birds of the heavens?'" (Job 35:9–11)

Elihu observes that when the oppressed feel trapped, they cry out to one stronger than themselves ("the arm of the mighty"). They want God's help to bring relief. But in their cries, they do not seek God himself. They are not seeking their Creator, just a deliverer. Because of a misaligned focus, their cries are unanswered: "There they cry out, but he does not answer, because of the pride of evil men. Surely God does not hear an empty cry, nor does the Almighty regard it" (Job 35:12–13).

Of course we are all inclined to avoid suffering. When it comes, we seek relief above all else. We are driven by our own desire for comfort. But God might have a greater plan than relief.

Let me be clear: it is not wrong to pray for relief. During his earthly ministry, people pleaded with Jesus for physical relief. Others pleaded for physical and spiritual relief from oppressive demons. And he granted those pleas. Sometimes our Lord delights in bringing an end to suffering. Indeed, bringing healing might be what most glorifies him in the moment. At other times, however, his design is different. Our prayers should reflect this understanding. It is, in fact, one of the ways in which living with incurable illness has led to spiritual growth in my own life.

I have written elsewhere about the moment my heart shifted from one seeking relief to one seeking his strength for the journey.[4] When it became clear that no medical intervention would bring relief to my incessant back pain, and the Lord had not brought relief through miraculous intervention, I did not know if I either could or wanted to live life in such pain. As my heart descended into the darkness of the moment, one verse kept coming to mind: "I can do all things through him who strengthens me" (Philippians 4:13). As I repeated that verse over and over, I sensed a resolve growing in my heart. I realized that yes, I can live with pain that never ends if that is God's plan for my life, because I will not face it in my own strength. What I needed was not relief, but a steadfast resolve that his strength will enable me to face this or any other trial. From that moment on, I stopped asking for relief. And when multiple sclerosis made its appearance later in my life, I never asked for healing (though others in my life have prayed to that end). I realized I don't need relief; I only need him and a heart that is molded by his will.

Again, I emphasize a point made earlier: it is not wrong to seek relief for yourself or others. But when such prayers are not answered over time, might it be that there is a higher priority for our prayers and for the prayers of those who pray for us?

QUALIFYING OUR APPEALS LIKE JESUS

No one has more clearly modeled a passionate appeal for relief, combined with a longing for God's will, than our Savior. In the midst of the agony provoked by his coming crucifixion, he cried out, "My Father, if it be possible, let this cup pass from me; nevertheless, not as I will, but as you will" (Matthew 26:39). This was not a wink at the end of his prayer or merely a gratuitous acknowledgment of who was in control of the moment. No, these words revealed the longing of Jesus's heart: that his Father's will be done. Even at great personal cost and indescribable suffering, he pursued the will of the Father. And we must do likewise.

But pursuing the will of the Father in the midst of suffering means more than adding a few special words at the end of our petitions for relief. It means truly believing that God might have a different outcome in mind. It means embracing the truth that our continued suffering could best fulfill his providential plan—and to be at peace with this.

Peace-filled acceptance of his providential plan means we don't rail at the injustice of it all, or whine about how hard we have it. Rather, we are content to live in his sovereign choice. In fact, it means preferring his will above our comfort. This might call for a pivot in our prayers.

I don't want to read too much into the text, but Jesus did not pray once in the Garden of Gethsemane and then walk away with a settled peace. No, he wrestled three times with a depth of agony none of us have ever known. Even though our trials, as difficult as they might be, will never compare to what Jesus endured, we also should not expect a settled peace to develop immediately in our hearts. Peace often arrives through a process. It is the fruit of toiling in our own garden of agony. Like real fruit, we cannot rush its ripening either in ourselves or in the lives of others. Remember that Job wrestled with God for a long time before he was comforted amid the ruins of his life.

While it is also hard to watch someone we love wrestle through the turmoil of a trial, we cannot—even dare not—try to shorten the journey for them with platitudes that won't help in the moment. But we can sit with them in the tempest and bring what comfort we are empowered to give. For it is God, and only God, who will do the heart work that ultimately leads to peace. Jesus wanted his disciples to watch *with* him, not to try to pull him out of the garden experience.

PURSUING GOD ABOVE ALL ELSE

When pain persists despite our appeals, I believe there is a better path for us to pursue than continuing our requests for relief. There comes a time to accept the seeming silence of heaven and turn to the passionate pursuit of growing *through* the trial and being used by God in that place of hardship, and even learning to rejoice in it. And yes, we can rejoice in hardship. The experience of the apostle Paul is instructive here:

> So to keep me from becoming conceited because of the surpassing greatness of the revelations, a thorn was given me in the flesh, a messenger of Satan to harass me, to keep me from becoming conceited. Three times I pleaded with the Lord about this, that it should leave me. But he said to me, "My grace is sufficient for you, for my power is made perfect in weakness." Therefore I will boast all the more gladly of my weaknesses, so that the power of Christ may rest upon me. For the sake of Christ, then, I am

> content with weaknesses, insults, hardships, persecutions, and calamities. For when I am weak, then I am strong. (2 Corinthians 12:7–10)

If I understand Paul correctly, he pleaded three times for relief, but no more. Jesus also prayed three times for the passing of the bitter cup. While I am not suggesting a specific numerical limit on the number of times or duration of asking for healing, it seems clear that there is a time to move on. Accept God's will and redirect your prayers. Paul could do this because he understood that weak vessels are the kind God especially uses to display his glory (2 Corinthians 4:7). Thus, he learned to be content in his weakness. And so can we.

But Paul learned to go beyond contentment in his suffering: "We rejoice in our sufferings, knowing that suffering produces endurance, and endurance produces character, and character produces hope, and hope does not put us to shame, because God's love has been poured into our hearts through the Holy Spirit who has been given to us" (Romans 5:3–5). Rejoicing in suffering—such a response seems unnatural, doesn't it? And it is. For it is produced by the Holy Spirit who dwells within us. His work in our hearts ultimately produces hope, which produces rejoicing. This is the blessing of pursuing God in the midst of suffering. It is coming to that place where we embrace his will as both producing our greatest good and his greater glory.

PUTTING IT INTO PRACTICE

How do we move from pursuing relief to pursuing God, especially in our prayers? Like many others, I have found the

Psalms to be the greatest source of help to guide my prayers. They direct my thoughts and affections Godward. Not just reading but memorizing and regularly reciting key psalms has been a practice that greatly benefits me, specifically in my pursuit of God himself. Years ago, I began using my morning work commute to recite Psalms. Each weekday, I rehearse a different group of psalms that provide a weekly reinforcement of those that I have put to memory. Of special help are those psalms that express a longing for God himself:

> O God, you are my God; earnestly I seek you;
> my soul thirsts for you;
> my flesh faints for you,
> as in a dry and weary land where there is no water.
> (Psalm 63:1)

> As a deer pants for flowing streams,
> so pants my soul for you, O God.
> My soul thirsts for God,
> for the living God.
> When shall I come and appear before God?
> (Psalm 42:1–2)

I have found, and trust you will as well, that such words set my focus for the day. Before my labors begin, my heart longing for God is expressed through the words of the psalmist. Whether you memorize and recite or simply read and meditate, the Psalter can draw your heart to streams of living water. It will both stimulate and quench your thirst for God. May you be like the psalmist who declared, "You have said, 'Seek my face.' My heart says to you, 'Your face, Lord, do I seek'" (Psalm 27:8).

QUESTIONS FOR REFLECTION AND APPLICATION

1. How has living with chronic illness impacted your prayer life? Write down and reflect on two ways your prayers have changed as a result of your illness.

2. When you pray for others who are living with an incurable illness, what do you ask God to do for them? Does this chapter help you think about specific things besides healing that you can pray for those who are suffering physically? Take some time now and pray for one or two people you know who are living with chronic illness.

3. Identify a psalm or portion of a psalm to memorize that will help you focus on the Lord and the value of pursuing him above all else.

Chapter 4

LEARNING OBEDIENCE THROUGH SUFFERING

Any trial can be to our benefit. But that does not mean the *purpose* of a trial is to root out something rotten in our lives. For example, Job's cruel calamities and loathsome sores were not intended to remove any idols from his heart. Indeed, it was his blameless character that brought about God's commendation and Satan's attack. Nevertheless, the testing that Satan intended for his ruin was ultimately to Job's benefit. Though he was a blameless man, the misery God allowed Satan to bring caused Job to gain a deeper understanding of and reverence for God (Job 42:5). Instead of turning him from God, his trial taught him to wholeheartedly turn toward God in unwavering trust.

Amazingly, even Jesus had something to learn through his terrible trial. His suffering reflected no shortcoming in his life. There was no sin that needed to be uprooted. He suffered for you and me—the innocent for the guilty. Yet Scripture tells us he learned through his suffering. How can that be? And how should it inform our experiences of suffering?

LEARNING IN HIS HUMANITY

The incarnation of Jesus is both marvelous and mysterious. Scripture declares that Jesus was God come in human flesh. The fullness of what this means is beyond the reach of our limited minds. In Jesus's deity, there was no deficiency. But in his humanity, he grew like you and me. Luke 2:52 tells us that the boy Jesus "increased in wisdom and in stature and in favor with God and man."

Jesus grew in wisdom. How can the one who brought the world into being gain wisdom? Doesn't that seem contrary to his divine nature? Yes, but it is not an unexpected element of his human nature. For all humans grow and mature through time and experience. Jesus did the same. But he was eternally begotten, one with the Father. Didn't he know everything? Yes, he did. So how could he have grown in wisdom?

I make no pretense to fully understand the incarnation, but Scripture does not support the notion that Jesus was somehow compartmentalized into two beings—sometimes acting through the divine side and other times through the human side. He was the eternal Son who became man. His deity and humanity were wedded in incomprehensible fashion. And as the God–man, he matured. Specifically, he gained wisdom. Wisdom is acquired when knowledge and experience combine to give insight. It is, I believe, this experiential element through which Jesus grew.

During my didactic and clinical training, I learned about chronic pain. In a diabetes clinic, I sought to help patients who lived with incessant nerve pain in their feet. I've subsequently taught about pain and its management in several universities. But it was not until I was struck with chronic pain myself that I truly understood the experience of patients who lived with pain 24/7/365. It is one thing to know about pain; it is another to experience it. I have similarly heard oncologists tell of how their own experience as a cancer patient enlightened them far beyond what their clinical training and practice provided. It is at least partly, though perhaps not exclusively, in this sense that Jesus grew through his earthly journey. He gained something that only experience could provide.

If Jesus grew through his suffering, can we not grow through ours? If the anticipation and agony of the cross was a path for learning for the eternal Son, might God also use our experience of living with chronic illness to grow us in ways unobtainable without such suffering? Coming to recognize what God can do in my life *through* suffering has been one of the most important facets of my own spiritual growth, and I believe it can be in yours as well. You can learn in the school of suffering.

JESUS GAINED SYMPATHY THROUGH TEMPTATION

The story of the temptation of Jesus in the wilderness is known to most people who have some familiarity with the Bible (see Matthew 4:1–11). By enduring these temptations without sin, Jesus proved his unwavering allegiance to the Father. No earthly pleasure or treasure could dissuade him from the Father's chosen path. This, and other experiences of temptation, equipped him to be of help to us in our times of temptation: "Because he himself [Jesus] has suffered when tempted, he is able to help those who are being tempted" (Hebrews 2:18).

The writer of Hebrews tells us that *because* he suffered through temptation, he is able to help us in our experience of temptation. Experiencing temptation—not just knowing about it—put Jesus in the position to be of special help to us.

He understands the tension of the testing, for he felt it in full force. Indeed, he felt it more deeply than you and me, for the tension of temptation is greatest when it is resisted, but it is relieved when we surrender to it. Jesus never gave in to temptation. Thus, he felt its full weight. Because of this, he can sympathize with our plight:

> Since then we have a great high priest who has passed through the heavens, Jesus, the Son of God, let us hold fast our confession. For we do not have a high priest who is unable to sympathize with our weaknesses, but one who in every respect has been tempted as we are, yet without sin. (Hebrews 4:14–15)

Jesus gained compassion for our experiences of temptation by personally experiencing temptation. It is not that he did not care prior to his incarnation. After all, it was his love for us that motivated him to temporarily empty himself of his heavenly exaltation, take on the form of a servant, and die on our behalf. He came into this sin-cursed world because he cared. But what he experienced on this earth gave him an incalculable measure of sympathy.

I have recounted elsewhere[5] the story of the first patient who said to me, "Doc, you don't know what it is like to live with a burning pain in the bottom of your foot that never goes away." He was right. I truly felt sorry for him and wanted to help. But having now lived with a burning pain in the bottom of my right foot for over fifteen years, I understand such patients more than ever. I have gained a greater sympathy. But I've also gained something else—I've gained credibility. When I speak to patients with chronic pain, they know that I know what they are experiencing. Not just intellectually, but experientially. Thus, when I engage people living with chronic pain, they are confident they will find a sympathetic ear.

Isn't it amazing that our Savior entered into our experience of suffering and temptation? Doesn't that assure us that he has a sympathetic ear? He is one who knows what we are going through. He knows what it feels like. He has walked the walk. When we come to him, he truly understands. Holding on to this comforting truth can also give us greater confidence in our prayers, a greater boldness to come to him.

JESUS WAS PERFECTED THROUGH SUFFERING

In addition to gaining sympathy, Jesus was also perfected through suffering: "For it was fitting that he, for whom and by whom all things exist, in bringing many sons to glory, should make the founder of their salvation perfect through suffering" (Hebrews 2:10). Does that verse give you pause? How could Jesus, the founder of our salvation, be made perfect? Wasn't he already perfect in his being?

We are inclined to think of perfection in contrast to imperfection, and that is sometimes the right understanding of the word. However, it is clear there was no imperfection in the sinless Son of God. The writer of Hebrews is not speaking of removing some stain from the Son's character. The Greek word translated *perfect* also carries the notion of completing or fulfilling something. Jesus fulfilled the purpose of his incarnation through his suffering. It was through this means that he completed the Father's charge and fully became the Savior of the world. Until he drank the bitter cup, his task was not done. His purpose was unfulfilled. His work was completed, or perfected, through his suffering.

Jesus came for a purpose. And that purpose could not be fully realized until he suffered. While it is true that his teachings revealed the Father as never before—and in themselves, they are of great benefit—he would not have become the founder of our salvation apart from the agony of Calvary. In this sense, he was truly perfected through suffering.

Similarly, something amazing occurred through Paul's bearing his thorn in the flesh. After Paul pleaded for relief, God said to him, "My grace is sufficient for you, for my power is made perfect in weakness" (2 Corinthians 12:9). Clearly, nothing is deficient in God's power. He is omnipotent. While it's admittedly hard to get our heads around the concept, Paul's weakness in suffering was a means of completing or perfecting the power of God! There is a way in which God's power is displayed in our times of physical weakness that is different from when it occurs apart from our weakness.

You see, our weakness is an avenue for God's glory in a way that few other experiences are. Knowing this, I can trust that God is working through me—and in me—even when I feel that my world is shrinking because of my physical limitations. For it is then that his power is especially displayed.

JESUS LEARNED OBEDIENCE THROUGH SUFFERING

The writer of Hebrews tells us that in suffering, Jesus did more than just complete his role as Savior. Through suffering he also learned obedience:

> In the days of his flesh, Jesus offered up prayers and supplications, with loud cries and tears, to him who was able to save him from death, and he was heard because of his reverence. Although he was a son, he learned obedience through what he suffered. And

> being made perfect, he became the source of eternal salvation to all who obey him. (Hebrews 5:7–9)

We are given few glimpses into the private prayer life of Jesus. The most moving are his appeals to the Father in the Garden of Gethsemane. This, I believe, is what the writer of Hebrews is referencing in the passage above. For his appeal was "to him who was able to save him from death." Clearly, the priority of his pleading was to escape the cruel cross. His appeals to the Father for an alternative path, one that would avoid the bitter cup, were agonizing. They brought about such an intensity of emotion that it was manifested by sweating great drops of blood. To say that Jesus wished to forestall the agony ahead would be an understatement. And yet, how did he qualify this urgent appeal? "Nevertheless, not my will, but yours, be done" (Luke 22:42).

Though his plea to avoid the cross was not granted, "he was heard because of his reverence." Meditate on that for a moment. His appeal was heard. Did the Father merely grasp the words spoken by his Son, or did he actually grant his appeal? Jesus knew to whom his request was directed. It was the Father, the one who holds all things in his hand. The one whose wisdom is unsearchable. The one who knows the end from the beginning. The one whose ways go beyond human understanding. Therefore, in reverence, in acknowledgment of who God is, Jesus declared, "Nevertheless, not my will, but yours, be done." He honored the Father in his prayer: "I want your will even if it means the path of suffering." And the Father granted that prayer.

In the hours ahead of the cross, Jesus experienced the fullness of what it means to obey the Father. He learned that obedience sometimes means suffering. It means choosing the hard road rather than the smooth path. It means embracing affliction rather than avoiding it. In doing so, as our elder brother, Jesus shows us the way forward in times of suffering.

WE CAN LEARN THROUGH JESUS'S EXAMPLE

Jesus's example, his response to suffering, teaches us some very important lessons. These lessons can enable us to avoid being crushed in the crucible of affliction. The first and most important lesson is that *suffering is ultimately for our gain*. We tend to focus on what is lost in trials, and the loss is very real. It might hurt deeply, as it did for Jesus. But seeking to avoid the loss or mourning it was not his greatest priority, nor should it be ours. Instead, like Jesus, we can focus on what is gained.

Jesus's focus was not on the suffering itself, but on what it would produce. That was the source of his joy (Hebrews 12:2). And we must also learn to turn our eyes and consider the gain that comes from suffering:

> And we know that for those who love God all things work together for good, for those who are called according to his purpose. For those whom he foreknew he also predestined to be conformed to the image of his Son, in order that he might be the firstborn among many brothers. And those whom he predestined he also called, and those whom he called he also justified, and those whom he justified he also glorified. (Romans 8:28–30)

We must never forget that everything the Father brings into our lives is molding us for glory, shaping us into the image of his dear Son. All suffering is ultimately for our good.

Second, *suffering should produce sympathy for others*. Serious suffering can cause us to be self-absorbed. Pain and sorrow tend to draw us inward. But it produced sympathy in

Jesus and should also do so in us. There are wounded ones all around us. Who can better understand their pain than fellow sufferers?

True sympathy moves beyond feelings. Sympathy, like love, should compel us to action. It should cause us to bring comfort where we can. Indeed, this is a responsibility entrusted to those who have been comforted in their trials:

> Blessed be the God and Father of our Lord Jesus Christ, the Father of mercies and God of all comfort, who comforts us in all our affliction, so that we may be able to comfort those who are in any affliction, with the comfort with which we ourselves are comforted by God. For as we share abundantly in Christ's sufferings, so through Christ we share abundantly in comfort too. (2 Corinthians 1:3–5)

The comfort we receive in our trials is "so that we may be able to comfort those who are in any affliction." We give to others what we have gained ourselves: comfort. We come alongside and strengthen them in their time of testing.

Those who live with chronic suffering must learn to navigate life as both a recipient *and* a giver of comfort. The magnitude of each will oscillate with our physical limitations. There will be times when our illness puts us in the place of being mostly a recipient, while at other times we will be enabled to give to others. But even in times of great physical limitations, we can seek to minister to others. I have watched believers in hospice care during the final stages of life turn their forced idleness to an opportunity for greater intercessory prayer.

Third, we embrace the truth that *suffering is the path the Father has charted for our lives*. He has the power to bring relief, just as he could have prevented it in the first place. Our suffering did not enter our lives by chance, nor is its continued presence the bad luck of the draw. It is the path the Father has paved for us. If we believe God is in control of all things, and I hope you do, then we know all that we experience is part of his sovereign plan. Apart from our suffering, we cannot fulfill his plan for us. Can you accept that? Can you embrace the reality that the Father's plan, wherever the journey takes you, is what fulfills his purpose for your life? Can you trust his choice, even when that choice involves pain and sorrow? Jesus did. And he invites you to do the same.

But Jesus does not ask us to walk a hard path alone. He did not just give us an example to follow, though that in itself would be a great help. He is also with us always. He has sent the Comforter, the Holy Spirit, who empowers us to do what we could not do in our own strength. The saving work of Jesus accomplishes more than meeting the demand of justice required by God's wrath toward sin. It also reaches into our daily lives through the presence of the Holy Spirit. He journeys with us, carrying us across the rough road of suffering. He has not only planned the path; he travels with us on it.

In John 14:18, Jesus assured the disciples, "I will not leave you as orphans; I will come to you." Jesus has not left us to face the travails of this life alone. In the person of the Spirit, he abides with us through every step of every trial. Because of this, we have help in our greatest moments of weakness. Romans 8:26 elaborates on the help we receive from the Spirit even in our struggle to pray: "In the same way, the Spirit helps us in our weakness. We do not know what we ought to pray for, but the Spirit himself intercedes for us through wordless groans."

Have you ever been there—distressed to the point where you don't even know how to pray? We are not alone in those moments. The Spirit who dwells within us intercedes for us. This truth should bring us great comfort.

QUESTIONS FOR REFLECTION AND APPLICATION

1. Trusting that God can work through our weaknesses is really hard. It can help to read the testimony of one who has walked through suffering and experienced this truth. To that end, read the testimony of Joni Eareckson Tada on the fiftieth anniversary of her diving accident that left her a paraplegic. Her testimony can be found at The Gospel Coalition website: https://www.thegospelcoalition.org/article/reflections-on-50th-anniversary-of-my-diving-accident/

2. Take some time to write down what God is teaching you through your experience(s) of physical suffering. How have you grown in your faith through affliction? Then share what you have learned with a loved one or your small group.

3. Read Genesis 50:15–21. How did Joseph view the hard trials that he faced as a result of his brothers' betrayal? What application might his experience have for your life?

Chapter 5

THE SPIRITUAL CHALLENGES OF LIVING WITH PERSISTENT SUFFERING

When suffering persists, it is easy to focus on the source of suffering—a physical ailment, past trauma, or an unwanted mental state such as depression. But all suffering, regardless of its cause, readily produces spiritual challenges. This is especially true with an ongoing physical illness or pain. While an acute illness threatens our health, a chronic illness threatens our self. Limitations on physical activity might impair our ability to work, participate in leisure activities, perform household chores, and even fulfill familial responsibilities. What were once seen as simple physical activities are now painful or avoided altogether. Our roles in life might be changed to such a degree that we might struggle with our personal and professional identity. We can no longer be all we expected to be as a spouse, parent, friend, or employee.

These changes, and their lasting impact on our lives, create spiritual challenges that must be recognized and addressed. If they are ignored, our walk with Jesus will be hindered. While the specific manifestations of spiritual struggle vary from one person to the next, I have found it helpful to see them in the context of four broad categories illustrated in Figure 2: guilt, anger, fear of man, and anxiety.

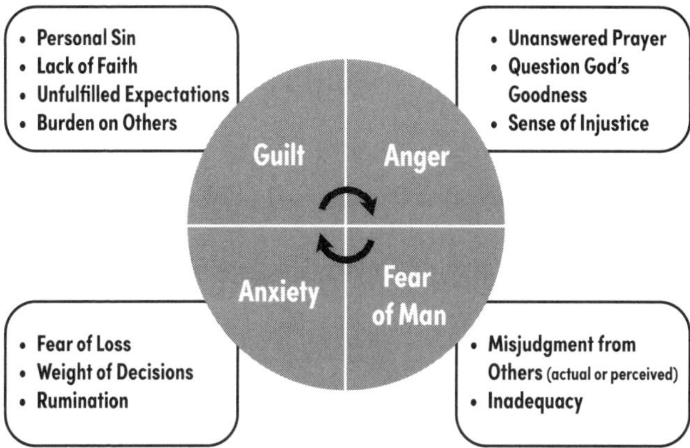

Figure 2. Summary of the Spiritual Challenges of Living with Persistent Suffering

RECOGNIZING AND RESPONDING TO FEELINGS OF GUILT

When suffering persists, especially in the face of fervent prayers for relief, sufferers will often ask if their distress is punishment for sin. This response is at least as old as the book of Job. As Job's three friends observed his ongoing suffering, they wrongly concluded its presence must be retribution for some sin in Job's life—otherwise, why would God allow him to suffer so? Likewise, many (perhaps most?) sufferers will at some point ask if their ongoing affliction has been caused by personal sin. As a consequence, they become gripped by guilt.

Guilt can be consuming. And when wrongly felt or responded to, it can distort our view of life's circumstances. But how can you tell if guilt has gripped your soul? Reflect on the following questions:

- Do you find yourself frequently rehearsing in your mind a past sin?
- Do you tend to view trouble in your life as punishment from God?
- Do you often feel ashamed when you come before God in prayer, even in the absence of some unconfessed sin?
- Do you feel your sin continues to be a barrier between you and God?
- Do you see yourself as unworthy of God's care and attention?

If these are true of you, it is likely that guilt has a hold on your heart. So you should ask if that sense of guilt is warranted. This is a necessary process, as misplaced guilt can be crushing.

There are examples in Scripture where personal sin has brought judgment in the form of physical illness. Miriam, the sister of Moses, was struck with a dreadful skin disease as judgment for speaking against Moses (Numbers 12). Some in the Corinthian church were struck ill because of partaking of the Lord's Table in an unworthy manner (1 Corinthians 11). Note that in each of these cases, the cause for their suffering (judgment from God) was clearly revealed. Their suffering was corrective for the sufferer and a warning for others not to follow their folly.

The Bible also teaches the principle of sowing and reaping (Galatians 6:7 and throughout the book of Proverbs). Some physical ailments (e.g., sexually transmitted diseases or injury incurred while driving drunk) might arise because we have violated the divine order of things in this world and bear the consequences (though sometimes those who suffer are innocent, and it is the sin of others that have brought the suffering). Sinful behavior can give rise to physical illness with long-lasting effects. Ungodly conduct can also create haunting memories and contribute to or worsen mental/emotional suffering such as depression or anxiety.

It is wise to prayerfully ask if sin has brought physical illness or is contributing to your mental health challenges. In the examples given above, there was a clear and obvious connection between sin and its consequences. If your personal interrogation of your life suggests that this is true for you as well, confess and repent where needed. Then walk in the confidence of the forgiveness promised (1 John 1:9). Do not continue to rehearse sin that has been forgiven. If there is no obvious connection, be wary of concocting one. Remember the error of the disciples of Jesus who thought the man was blind from birth because of sin in his or his parents' lives (John 9:1–5). You don't want to repeat their error. You might find it helpful to walk through your thought processes with a pastor or trusted counselor.

Even if you rightly conclude your affliction is due to personal sin, repentance does not assure healing. David pleaded in deep contrition for the life of his infant son from Bathsheba, yet the child died (2 Samuel 12:15–23). Forgiveness does not always prevent temporal consequences. A dear friend who was an addict experienced a stroke after injecting an illegal drug. Waking up in the hospital and seeing the train wreck his life had become, he repented and gave his life to Christ. But his walking remains impaired from the stroke he experienced decades earlier. His soul was healed, but his body was not—and he is at peace with that reality because he is now at peace with God.

In trials arising from physical illness, it is important to realize that most illness is *not* judgment for specific sin. In the accounts of Jesus healing people, he did not call individuals to repent before healing. Nor did the apostles tell people to repent before they healed them in Jesus's name. Consider also that Paul exhorted Timothy to use a little wine for his stomach ailment, rather than called him to repent (1 Timothy 5:23). For most, there is no connection between illness and sin apart from the unbroken chain that links all suffering in this world to the original sin of Adam and Eve (see Genesis 3).

Some wrongly conclude that their ongoing suffering is penance for past sin. They live with unresolved guilt over past sin and link the development of a persistent problem to God exacting a price for their wrongdoing. This is a mistaken view of how God deals with his children. God *does not* impose retribution or penance for sin paid for by his beloved Son. If you are a follower of Jesus, the price has been paid for your sin—all of it!

The record of debt against us and the just penalty for our sin have been canceled (Colossians 2:13–14). Jesus set these aside by his death on the cross. Therefore, there is no longer a debt or penalty to be paid. God will not require payment or impose a penalty for a debt from which his Son has already set us free. Do not, my Christian friend, allow past sins to haunt you. Whatever pain or sorrow you might bear today is not some form of retribution from the hand of our heavenly Father.

While there are natural consequences to violating the divine order God has created in this world, we should not view these consequences as God's direct retribution for sin. As beautifully described in Genesis 1 and 2, our Lord created a good world in which humans could flourish as his image bearers. He created a cycle to the movement of stars and planets in the heavens, as well as seasons and tides on the earth. The entrance of sin disrupted the divine order of things, which brought pain, sorrow, and death. Much of the suffering we see and experience arises from the simple fact that we live in a broken world. The physical suffering from pandemics and natural disasters arises from this disordered world.

Likewise, when we violate God's order in our individual lives through personal sin, there are often consequences—not as direct judgment, but because we have violated the divine order of things. If I sinfully ignore the speed limit while driving (as well as defying the laws of physics) by racing my car through a curve, I should not be surprised if I bear physical suffering as a result. If I engage in sexually promiscuous behavior, I should not be surprised if I contract a sexually transmitted disease. These are natural consequences of defying the order of things, not God exacting specific retribution for my folly.

Sadly, some who endure ongoing suffering will be told by others that the Lord would heal them if they just had enough faith. By misapplying Scripture passages, people who profess to follow Jesus assault sufferers with assurance that healing will come if they just muster up enough faith. When healing does not come, guilt about their lack of faith adds to their suffering. In other words, sufferers might see their ongoing affliction as evidence of their own lack of faith, which only adds to their sense of guilt (e.g., "I continue to suffer because my faith is weak").

The false teaching that faith always brings healing denies the clear biblical teaching that suffering is to be expected in this life. Jesus told his disciples, "I have said these things to you, that in me you may have peace. In the world you will have tribulation. But take heart; I have overcome the world" (John 16:33).

Was the persistence of Paul's thorn in the flesh a result of his lack of faith? No, it was because God had a higher purpose for his suffering (2 Corinthians 12:1–10). Was the sickness of

Lazarus that led to his death evidence of his lack of faith? No, it was that Jesus might be glorified through his miraculous resurrection (John 11:1–4).

Here is a simple truth: those who claim that faith always overcomes illness all meet the same end—death. Their deception is demonstrated by their own demise. Let no one saddle you with the false guilt that your ongoing suffering is the result of inadequate faith. Those who would tell you this are cruel counselors akin to Job's friends (Job 16:2).

Perhaps even more pervasive are feelings of guilt by sufferers because they cannot meet their own expectations or those of others. When your ailment impairs your ability to be all that you think a spouse should be, you might feel guilty about your inability. Sufferers might feel guilty that their spouse has to bear the burden of their illness, whether that's assuming added responsibilities or dealing with limitations on what physical activity they can share as a couple. Guilt might strike you when you miss important events in your children's lives because of chronic illness. And guilt is a common response when your ailments keep you from expected work duties.

Those living with chronic illness must recognize that there is no need for guilt about things over which they have no control. You did not choose illness and are not at fault for the situation. It is okay to express regret to others for the limitations that exist because of illness, as well as sorrow that things are not as you hoped they would be. But you owe no apology to anyone for an illness that you did not choose. It is also important to realize that the experience of your loved ones is under the same providential control of God as is your experience with chronic illness. Just as the Lord has a purpose for your chronic ailment, he also has a purpose for the burden others might bear because of your affliction. In the same way he uses your ailment to refine you, he can use the burden of being a caregiver to refine those who care for you.

The limitations imposed by an enduring affliction can readily give rise to feelings of guilt. We must recognize this tendency and address it directly. We must battle against false guilt with the truth of Scripture. False guilt will rob us of joy and dim the light of Christ that should shine through us.

RECOGNIZING AND RESPONDING TO ANGER

Why is this happening to me? This is the common cry of those living with an unending trial. And it is not wrong to ask why. Nor is it wrong to passionately express your anguish to God. As discussed in Chapter 1, the Psalms provide many examples of lament—a process through which we move from turmoil to trust despite the ongoing adversity.

But a persistently questioning heart is in danger of becoming an angry heart. As we see others free from such limitations, we might conclude that we have gotten a raw deal from God. Like Job, we might believe we have been treated unjustly by the God who controls all things. Dwelling in this state for too long can lead us to question God's goodness and feel angry toward him, which will turn into bitterness if left unaddressed. It is with good reason that we are warned, "Do not let the sun go down on your anger" (Ephesians 4:26). Like our Lord, we should feel anger toward injustice and other forms of evil. Such anger can move us to relieve the affliction of the oppressed and protect the innocent. But anger at our lot in life and the afflictions that trouble us is not a righteous anger. And anger directed toward God and his sovereign choices in our lives is a dangerous state of being. Persisting in such a state is a danger to our spiritual well-being.

Festering anger gives rise to bitterness, and bitterness is cancerous to the human soul. Left to grow, it will ruin us. This is why the Bible contains warnings such as this: "See to it that no one fails to obtain the grace of God; that no 'root of bitterness' springs up and causes trouble, and by it many become defiled" (Hebrews 12:15).

Like a cancer in our physical bodies, anger and bitterness need to be recognized and removed. But how can we tell if we are in the grip of anger and bitterness? Here are some common signs:

- a lack of joy
- minor inconveniences provoke an angry outburst
- one is easily irritated by others
- a tendency to see the worst in events or others
- regularly replaying offenses in your mind
- an unwillingness to forgive others
- questioning the goodness of God

If these signs are present in your life, you need to spend time in prayerful soul-searching. Ask the Lord to reveal the state of your heart, specifically whether anger and bitterness have gripped your soul.[6]

How can we expel anger or bitterness that resides in our souls? First, we must recognize the root of ungodly anger/bitterness. They arise when we live by the flesh: "Now the works of the flesh are evident: sexual immorality, impurity, sensuality, idolatry, sorcery, enmity, strife, jealousy, *fits of anger*, rivalries, dissensions, divisions" (Galatians 5:19–20, emphasis added). The presence of sinful anger and bitterness reveals that we are being driven by the flesh and not the Spirit. The proper response is to confess it to God, and to others where appropriate (James 5:16; 1 John 1:9). Then we must commit to turning from it (Ephesians 4:31).

We must resolve to banish sinful anger from our hearts. The way to empty our minds of sinful ways of thinking is to fill them with solid scriptural truth. Paul told the Colossians to "put to death therefore what is earthly in you" (Colossians 3:5). The way to do this is to "let the word of Christ dwell in you richly, teaching and admonishing one another in all wisdom, singing psalms and hymns and spiritual songs, with thankfulness in your hearts to God" (Colossians 3:16). Elsewhere, he instructs, "Whatever is true, whatever is honorable, whatever is just, whatever is pure, whatever is lovely, whatever is commendable, if there is any excellence, if there is anything worthy of praise, think about these things" (Philippians 4:8). Our minds often serve as the gateway to our heart. In other words, heart change often arises from changing the focus of our thinking.

Trials will either make us bitter or better. How we respond in a time of testing will determine which of these possible outcomes prevail. We must realize that trials are both a threat and an opportunity. They are a threat in that the enemy of our souls seeks to use them to turn us from God, as he attempted to do with Job. They are also an opportunity to prove our faith, both to ourselves and to those who watch us endure a trial. In other words, trials present us with the opportunity to glorify God in the midst of our suffering. Living through such tests of faith with patient endurance manifests the power of Christ in us. In this way, we can honor him through a world of hurt.

The power of Christ is also displayed when we turn from bitterness to trust. If we have allowed ourselves to be gripped with anger festering into bitterness, rooting out the bitterness and replacing it with patient endurance in the midst of a trial is a powerful testimony to a watching world of the ability of Christ to transform lives. Yes, even when we have given way to sinful ways of thinking, the Lord can use us as a light to the world by showing his gracious work when his children struggle through hard times. Seeing how we deal with those times when our hearts have gone astray can help others understand what it means to walk with Jesus in a broken world.

RECOGNIZING AND RESPONDING TO THE FEAR OF MAN

There is probably too much fear of man in all of us. When we fear man, we are inordinately concerned about how others judge us. Who among us has not felt this way, at one time or another? The fear of man can be an even more frequent struggle for those who live with an enduring affliction.

People living with chronic illness are frequently judged by others. Others might see them as being lazy or antisocial because they avoid certain activities. Many people struggle with an ailment that is essentially invisible to others (e.g., chronic pain). They "look okay" but are actually plagued by debilitating symptoms. It is common for people to spend years going to a variety of specialists seeking an answer to the troubling symptoms they experience—and they often end up with uncertain diagnoses. This uncertainty and invisibility lead others, including family members and friends, to question the validity of their complaints. These all conspire to cause people living with chronic illness to fear what others think of them, and it can become a consuming fear.

I often find myself in a setting where men are asked to do something physical, such as carrying tables or chairs or carrying heavy items from one place to another. But my physical ailments make it unwise for me to comply with such requests. Yet if I don't do so, others might wonder why I am not helping. I have to fight the inclination to give in to the fear of man and do what I know I should not do, just to prevent others from thinking poorly of me.

How can we tell if we are plagued with the fear of man? Consider these questions:

- Are you embarrassed by your physical limitations?
- Do you crave the approval of others?
- Do you struggle with feelings of inadequacy?
- Do you try to hide your weaknesses?
- Are you unwilling to share your struggles with others?

If these are true of you, it is likely that you are gripped by the fear of man. This is a fate that Scripture warns us to avoid: "The fear of man lays a snare, but whoever trusts in the Lord is safe" (Proverbs 29:25).

Living in the fear of man is like falling into a trap. Isn't that a powerful picture? Our spiritual well-being will be endangered. But how do we defeat this tendency? The first step is to acknowledge that we struggle with it. Second, we must recognize that God works through our weaknesses: "But he said to me, 'My grace is sufficient for you, for my power is made perfect in weakness.' Therefore I will boast all the more gladly of my weaknesses, so that the power of Christ may rest upon me" (2 Corinthians 12:9).

Can we, like Paul, see that our weaknesses actually display the power of Christ? Can we rejoice that our weaknesses create an opportunity for his grace to shine through us? Paul's words turn the ways of men on their head. It is not through human strength that God is most honored. It is through weak vessels.

This is a truth we must preach to ourselves when the fear of man raises its ugly head in our hearts. It matters little what men might think of us. Paul, who seemed to be incessantly judged by others, understood this well: "But with me it is a very small thing that I should be judged by you or by any human court. In fact, I do not even judge myself" (1 Corinthians 4:3). Paul was concerned about no one's judgment but God's. We would do well to follow his example.

RECOGNIZING AND RESPONDING TO ANXIETY

When living with an incurable illness or other form of ceaseless tribulation, it is easy to give way to anxiety. We can become consumed with worry about what the future holds and how we will cope. We might fear the loss of things dear to us and struggle with the weight of hard decisions. Some sufferers spend much time ruminating on what has been lost and how that has changed their life, as well as where it will lead in the days ahead.

How can you tell if you have developed an anxious heart? Reflect on these questions:

- Does thinking about your future produce fear?
- When you think about the future, do you focus on the added loss that might come?
- Do you find it hard to enjoy the present and instead find your mind wandering to worries about what new physical limitations will develop?
- When social events draw near, do you find yourself thinking about what could go wrong?
- Do you often come up with excuses to avoid attending group gatherings (church, dinners, etc.)?

Those living with increasing physical limitations often become socially isolated. This leads to idle time that used to be filled with meaningful activities. As a result, their mind increasingly focuses on all that has been lost through illness and what further losses might lie ahead. Those with trauma, depression, or other mental/emotional challenges might withdraw to avoid additional hurt. Regardless of the cause, isolation sets the stage for anxious thoughts to consume a person.

When you recognize that you are struggling with anxiety in response to your suffering, you must guard against isolation. Anxiety not only causes us to retreat, but retreating from others also makes our worries worse. The Lord has made us to thrive in community, especially the community of the local church. Withdrawing from fellowship endangers our spiritual well-being. It is easy to become like Job by spending too much time in our own heads and convincing ourselves of untrue things.

Job began strong, affirming his confidence in God's control (Job 1 and 2). But as his suffering continued, he was isolated from friends and family. He was a pitiful outcast in a society that saw suffering as a sign of God's disfavor. Then, after sitting for seven days in silence with his newly arrived friends, Job burst out with a wish that he had never been born, or at least that his life would end (Job 3). He moved from standing strong in his faith when trouble first struck to being in deep despair, for he focused on his trouble rather than the Lord who would see him through his turmoil. As the narrative of Job continues, it reveals just how distorted his view of God had become. He came to believe that God had turned against him (Job 6).

Wise friends can help us in troubled times. They can speak truth to our anxious hearts. Of course, as Job learned, it is also true that sometimes friends bring harm rather than help. And if this has happened to us, we will be especially anxious about sharing our troubles with others, out of fear of the response. But as the New Testament epistles reveal, living life with other Christians will be complicated. Even those who love us will sometimes say or do things that hurt. We must not allow these difficulties to cause us to shrink back from fellowship. For along with the difficult part of the relationships is the blessing of supporting and comforting one another. We must accept the bad with the good that comes from community life in the local church. When on the receiving end of thoughtless or hurtful words from others, I find it helpful to remind myself that I have too often done the same. Thus, I can show the grace I need myself.

Most often, we should let words that hurt roll off our back like water on a duck. Such a response is living out the call to be forgiving one another as Christ has forgiven us (Ephesians 4:32). But when it becomes a pattern within a community of believers, it may need to be addressed. In my experience, such words usually arise because people don't know what to say. After the death of our beloved son, my wife and I received some truly hurtful communications from members of our church (and from believers outside our church). At the same time, a dear friend with a diagnosis of terminal cancer had similarly unfortunate conversations with members of the congregation. I shared these struggles with one of our pastors. In response, he asked me to address the congregation on how to speak to those experiencing loss so we could all learn what to say and what to avoid in difficult times.

Even if other believers sometimes fail us, those who suffer would do well to remember how much God cares for us. In the Sermon on the Mount, Jesus assures his listeners that their heavenly Father knows about and will provide for their needs (Matthew 6:25–33). On the basis of this assurance, Jesus says, "Therefore do not be anxious about tomorrow, for tomorrow will be anxious for itself. Sufficient for the day is its own trouble" (Matthew 6:34). Instead of being consumed by thinking about the *what ifs* the future might hold, Jesus wants us to focus on being faithful today.

None of us can know what lies ahead, where our path in life will take us. But we can rest assured that our heavenly Father will provide for our needs. He will not abandon us. Recognizing this, we should heed the call of Paul:

> The Lord is at hand; do not be anxious about anything, but in everything by prayer and supplication with thanksgiving let your requests be made known to God. And the peace of God, which surpasses all understanding, will guard your hearts and your minds in Christ Jesus. (Philippians 4:5b–7)

KEEPING SPIRITUAL CHALLENGES IN PERSPECTIVE

Like Paul, we must be aware of Satan's devices (2 Corinthians 2:11). He will seek to use protracted trials to ruin us, as was his strategy with Job. The fallen world can deceive us with messages of hope that are, at best, bandages that merely cover up the trouble in our souls. Moreover, the weakness of our own flesh can draw us down a dangerous path.

Some of the challenges that sufferers most commonly face are guilt, anger, fear of man, and anxiety. But by the power of the Spirit and with the truth of the Word, we can live victoriously over these spiritual challenges. In the face of darkness, God's light can shine through us.

QUESTIONS FOR REFLECTION AND APPLICATION

1. Which of the four main spiritual challenges (guilt, anger, fear of man, anxiety) do you struggle with the most? Write down practical steps you can take to intentionally fight your inclination to give in to this area of struggle. Review this list of practical steps at the beginning of each week for the next month to remind you to put these into practice.

2. Studies have shown that caregivers (e.g., spouses, adult children) of people living with chronic illness often experience more depression and anxiety than the people for whom they care. Find a time to have an open conversation with your spouse or other caregiver about the impact of your illness on their life. Be sure to pray about this in your prayers for them.

Chapter 6

THE TREASURE OF PATIENT ENDURANCE

Like most people, I am inclined to avoid or alleviate pain rather than endure it. In my professional life, I have trained aspiring health professionals of all sorts on how to treat pain so patients can experience relief. Yet we all know that acute pain serves a useful purpose. Pain warns us to act to prevent further harm (e.g., pulling our hand away from a hot item) and alerts us to an injury that needs care. From a physical perspective, pain that endures seems to serve no purpose. Viewing suffering as pointless can have profound consequences.

In America, the highest rate of suicide occurs in people over 65 years of age.[7] The fact that the elderly are the demographic with the highest suicide rate usually surprises people. But this is also the age group with the highest rate of chronic illness that produces suffering. And most people see nothing to be gained by their continued suffering. But there is fruit to be born spiritually.

In my own life, the Lord has used the physical limitations of my ailments to strike a blow to my tendency toward self-sufficiency and pride. While evidence of both remains painfully present in my life, the need to rely on others to help or to refrain from some forms of activity is a constant reminder of my need for God's grace moment by moment.

The pulverizing impact of a sculptor's hammer and chisel ultimately reveals a beauty none but the artist could perceive in advance. The scorching heat of a refiner's fire burns away dross to produce purer metal. Similarly, believers who understand the heart work accomplished by trials will see their refining work as a gift from God. In bringing the trial, he is not doing something to us, but he is doing something in us and through us. And what he does brings blessing.

We can, however, miss the reality of blessing if we hold a distorted view of its meaning. It is, I believe, a mistake to equate *blessed* with *happy*. Happiness is an emotional state. But Jesus was speaking of something deeper than our feelings in the Beatitudes (Matthew 5:2–11). Nor does blessing primarily manifest itself with material goods, though God certainly blessed people like Abraham with riches. To be blessed means to have God's favor shine upon you. That favor is sometimes seen in the here and now, while at other times its evidence will be manifested in the future.

Empowered by the Holy Spirit, Elizabeth declared Mary to be blessed among women (Luke 1:42). Yet the mother of Jesus remained poor, was viewed with disdain by some because of her out-of-wedlock pregnancy, and bore the agony of watching her son crucified. Nonetheless, God's favor was upon her because through her came the Savior of the world (Luke 1:46–55). Neither earthly riches nor the favor of men was the means of her blessing. Rather, it was knowing her place in the redemptive plan of God. And through the millennia since, the people of God have acknowledged the blessing of her role in God's grand design. God's favor was upon her.

THE PROMISE OF BLESSING THROUGH TRIALS

When God makes a promise, you can be sure it will be fulfilled. Scripture assures us that there is blessing for those who remain steadfast in the face of trials: "Blessed are those who are persecuted for righteousness' sake, for theirs is the kingdom of heaven. Blessed are you when others revile you and persecute you and utter all kinds of evil against you falsely on my account. Rejoice and be glad, for your reward is great in heaven, for so they persecuted the prophets who were before you" (Matthew 5:10–12).

Persecution is one form of trial, one that most clearly identifies us with Jesus. And he promises blessing when we suffer specifically because we are his. There is great reward for those who suffer for Jesus's sake. But there is also promised blessing in other types of trials. For trials are always tests of our faith: "Blessed is the man who remains steadfast under trial, for when he has stood the test he will receive the crown of life, which God has promised to those who love him" (James 1:12).

Those who remain steadfast when tested will receive the crown of life. Crowns are given to those in privileged positions. Trials prepare us for the privileged place of reigning with Jesus. They refine us to be at his side. But our response is crucial when we're in the crucible of affliction. The blessing is promised to those who not just experience trials, but remain steadfast through the trial. As Paul told Timothy, "If we endure, we will also reign with him" (2 Timothy 2:12).

Sadly, there are also those who bail on Jesus in the face of testing. Perhaps, like me, you have met those who have turned from the faith because of their own suffering or through watching a loved one suffer. Seeing their suffering as pointless, they profess their inability to believe in a God who would allow such suffering. But it should not surprise us when people fail the test of trials and turn their back on God. In fact, in the parable of the sower and soils, Jesus told us that some would turn their back on him as a result of trials and tribulations (Matthew 13:1–23). Indeed, the writer of Hebrews warns those in the midst of trials not to turn from the faith:

> But recall the former days when, after you were enlightened, you endured a hard struggle with sufferings, sometimes being publicly exposed to reproach and affliction, and sometimes being partners with those so treated. For you had compassion on those in prison, and you joyfully accepted the plundering of your property, since you knew that you yourselves had a better possession and an abiding one. Therefore do not throw away your confidence, which has a great reward. (Hebrews 10:32–35)

Trials of every sort are a test of our faith. Just as fire tests the purity of gold, trials test the purity of our profession. The writer of Hebrews speaks with confidence that he and his readers are not among those who shrink back, who bail on Jesus when tested. But there are some who renounce Christ when struck by calamity. They desire relief above all else. To escape the suffering, they turn their back and abandon the faith. They "shrink back and are destroyed" (Hebrews 10:39).

Others turn on God in anger. When a hardship continues unabated, they rage against the injustice of their suffering: *How could God let this happen to me?* In their anguish, they convince themselves that God has abandoned them. So they abandon God. They turn from him instead of to him.

There might also be those who, while not turning from God, are robbed of joy and fruitfulness through their response to suffering. Such was the path of Job. The slow grind of pain wore him down. In his despondency, he lost the joy of what remained and could only mourn the loss. The constant misery he experienced became the focus of his life. He never lost his confidence in God's rule in his life, but he felt himself ill-treated and destined to dark days. This one who had been such a light for righteousness in the land of Uz, and who stood firmly in faith early on, gave way to despair. His hopelessness became plain for all to see.

I have seen believers wallow in self-pity over their suffering. Others take their frustrations out on those who love them most. They have allowed themselves to be mastered by their feelings, rather than using the trial to learn how to master their feelings.

How do we avoid such responses when testing comes? How do we remain on the path of blessing through the trial?

THE PATH TO BLESSING THROUGH TRIALS

James makes it clear that the great need in any trial is steadfastness, for this is the path to blessing. But what does this mean? In the Old Testament, the word *steadfast* is used to modify expressions of God's love several hundred times. Here are just a few examples:

- "Help me, O Lord my God! Save me according to your steadfast love!" (Psalm 109:26).
- "Give thanks to the God of heaven, for his steadfast love endures forever" (Psalm 136:26).
- "Who is a God like you, pardoning iniquity and passing over transgression for the remnant of his

> inheritance? He does not retain his anger forever, because he delights in steadfast love" (Micah 7:18).

To have steadfast love is to have a love that never lets go. It is a love that endures; it remains through thick and thin. Like the Rock of Gibraltar, it is unmovable. This is the nature of God's love for us. Isn't this an amazing truth?

From a human perspective, I have given the Lord countless reasons to withdraw his love from me. I presume the same is true for you. But his love for us remains steadfast. Though I might feel adrift in the storms of life, the anchor of his steadfast love forever holds. Knowing this, I can cling to him. And as I do so, I am held by one who will never let go.

Our ability to be steadfast is rooted in our confidence in being held in the Father's hand. This confidence was at the core of Paul's ability to stand fast in the most trying of circumstances. He declared, "For I know whom I have believed, and I am convinced that he is able to guard until that day what has been entrusted to me" (2 Timothy 1:12).

What enables believers to be steadfast in the midst of trials? What gives us the strength to hold fast and not lose our grip? *Hope*. It is hope that enables us to cling to the faith when pressed on every side. Hope is the anchor that holds us fast in the storms of life. We are encouraged in Hebrews 6 that

> we who have fled for refuge might have strong encouragement to hold fast to the hope set before us. We have this as a sure and steadfast anchor of the soul, a hope that enters into the inner place behind the curtain, where Jesus has gone as a forerunner on our behalf, having become a high priest forever after the order of Melchizedek. (vv. 18–20)

What enables us to hold fast in the face of adversity is the "hope set before us." It is a hope rooted in the finished work of Christ on our behalf. Our forerunner has gone before and will return to bring us to his Father's house (John 14:1–3). Come what may, we know Jesus will come for us. That is our hope, the sure anchor of our soul to which we hold through all affliction. It is what gives us the strength to endure. Knowing this, we patiently wait for his return: "Be patient, therefore, brothers, until the coming of the Lord. See how the farmer waits for the precious fruit of the earth, being patient about it, until it receives the early and the late rains. You also, be patient. Establish your hearts, for the coming of the Lord is at hand" (James 5:7–8).

Perhaps one reason we struggle through trials is that we do not think enough about Jesus's return—not the events surrounding his return, but the one who will return. The one who bought us with his precious blood. Our beloved Savior. Both our longing and our sure hope for his return give us the means to endure. But there's more. The trials themselves actually produce within us steadfastness. In other words, the steadfastness we need in the face of trials is also the fruit of trials.

THE FRUIT OF PATIENT ENDURANCE

"Count it all joy, my brothers, when you meet trials of various kinds, for you know that the testing of your faith produces steadfastness. And let steadfastness have its full effect, that you may be perfect and complete, lacking in nothing" (James 1:2–4). Do you see what James tells us here? Testing produces steadfastness. The various kinds of trials that enter our lives are producing within us the steadfastness we need to endure the trials.

When the first of three incurable ailments made its appearance in my life, the struggle was hard. Years of struggle, in fact. Most of all, I struggled because I focused on the physical problem. It took time for me to recognize the fundamental spiritual challenge it presented. As I began to see it in that light, my heart was molded in new directions. When a second ailment decided to join the journey, I more quickly saw the spiritual work it could produce. When the trifecta was completed, I was able to give limited thought to the physical and focus primarily on the spiritual elements. My prior growth prepared me for the latest affliction. When further curable afflictions arrived, I was better prepared to endure lengthy treatment and recovery periods.

You see, every trial prepares us for the next testing of our faith. As we learn through periods of testing, we are more fit to face future affliction. And ultimately, it prepares us for heaven—making us "perfect and complete, lacking in nothing." Can you see? In times of testing, God is not doing something to harm us; he is doing something to refine us. In other words, he is not leading us to ruin; he is leading us to glory. He is perfecting us for the day he calls us home.

James asks us to consider how this worked out in the lives of others, especially one of the most protracted examples of human suffering in Scripture: "As an example of suffering and patience, brothers, take the prophets who spoke in the name of the Lord. Behold, we consider those blessed who remained steadfast. You have heard of the steadfastness of Job, and you have seen the purpose of the Lord, how the Lord is compassionate and merciful" (James 5:10–11).

James encourages his readers to "Be patient . . . until the coming of the Lord" (James 5:7) by reminding them of the examples of the prophets. They often endured severe hardship. But they remained steadfast. Then there was Job. Even in the depth of darkness, he never wavered in his absolute confidence that God was in control. All Job experienced was from God's hand. And his steadfastness, not turning from the Lord but earnestly seeking him in the pain, was rewarded with a special appearance from the Lord himself. In the end, his steadfastness was rewarded (Job 42:10–17).

Just as he did in Job's life, God will accomplish his purposes through our times of testing. That does not mean it will be easy. Jesus showed us that the road of suffering can be deeply distressing. But he is with us through it all. Because of his promised presence, we can know the fullness of joy he promised—even when the hurt won't heal.

QUESTIONS FOR REFLECTION AND APPLICATION

1. Write down the two or three most important truths about suffering that you learned through reading this book. How will they help you in your own journey? Consider sharing your conclusions with your spouse or other family members.

2. Many people struggle with why God allows suffering. As a person who suffers from an illness, how would you answer if asked by someone who is struggling with this question?

ENDNOTES

1. This chapter is an expanded and modified version of the author's blog post at Faith Biblical Counseling Ministries, "A First Aid Kit for Dark Days," February 8, 2022, https://blogs.faithlafayette.org/counseling/2022/02/a-first-aid-kit-for-dark-days/.

2. "Belgic Confession," Christian Reformed Church (website), accessed February 18, 2024, https://www.crcna.org/welcome/beliefs/confessions/belgic-confession#toc-article-13-the-doctrine-of-god-s-providence.

3. For a meditative reflection on the experience of Job and what it teaches us about persistent suffering, see the author's book, *The Humbling of Job: Meditations on Finding Comfort Through Affliction* (West Lafayette, IN: Consilium Publishing, 2023).

4. Craig K. Svensson, *When There Is No Cure: How to Thrive While Living with the Pain and Suffering of Chronic Illness* (West Lafayette, IN: Consilium Publishing, 2018), pp. 204–205.

5. Svensson, *When There Is No Cure.*

6. For a helpful guide on identifying and dealing with bitterness, see Stephen Viars, *Overcoming Bitterness: Moving from Life's Greatest Hurts to a Life Filled with Joy* (Grand Rapids, MI: Baker Books, 2021).

7. Vital Statistics Rapid Release, Centers for Disease Control and Prevention, Report No. 34, November 2023, https://www.cdc.gov/nchs/data/vsrr/vsrr034.pdf.